Happy
Mothers Day
Mom!
Love,
Trish ♡
Chris
and
Stacey

A Special Gift

Presented to:

....

From:

....

Date:

....

Stories, Sayings, and Scriptures to Encourage and Inspire

hugs
for
Mom

HOWARD
PUBLISHING CO.

West Monroe, Louisiana

Our purpose at Howard Publishing is to:

- *Increase faith* in the hearts of growing Christians
- *Inspire holiness* in the lives of believers
- *Instill hope* in the hearts of struggling people
  everywhere

Because He's coming again!

Hugs for Mom
© 1997 by Howard Publishing Co., Inc.
All rights reserved

Published by Howard Publishing Co., Inc.,
3117 North 7th Street, West Monroe, LA 71291-2227

Printed in the United States of America

97 98 99 00 01 02 03 04 05 06   10 9 8 7 6 5 4 3

Stories by John William Smith, author of *My Mother's Favorite Song, My Mother Played the Piano,* and contributor to other *Hugs* books

Scriptures paraphrased by LeAnn Weiss, owner of Encouragement Company, Orlando, Florida

Jacket Design and Interior Art by LinDee Loveland
Edited by Philis Boultinghouse

The previous printing was catalogued as follows:

Library of Congress Cataloging-in-Publication Data

Hugs for the heart for mom : stories, sayings, and scriptures
to encourage and inspire.
       p. cm.
    ISBN 1-878990-69-1
     1. Mothers—Religious life. 2. Motherhood—
Religious aspects—Christianity. I. Howard Publishing Co.
BV4529.H84 1997
248.8'431—dc21
                                 97-681
                                    CIP

contents

one

nurturing hearts

*C*ultivate faith, goodness, knowledge, self-control, perseverance, godliness, brotherly kindness, and love in your children. For if they are growing in these qualities, they won't be ineffective or unproductive, and they will never stumble.

Love,

Your Living God

2 Peter 1:5–11

Jeremiah 10:10

You may not realize it, but *you* are a gifted gardener. Though you may be incapable of keeping a simple houseplant alive, you are an accomplished gardener nonetheless. The soil you work in is not of this world. No! It is the soil of the human heart.

Your children are your fertile field, and in their hearts you have tenderly planted your seeds of love, joy, peace, patience, kindness, goodness, faithfulness, gentleness, and self-control.

At times, you have courageously protected your precious field from destructive and uninvited strangers. When spiritual or physical disease threatened, you worked with bleeding hands to free the roots of life from contaminants. You have nursed the wounds left by the violent storms of life. You have struggled through seasons of drought; you have celebrated at the sight of unhampered growth. You have weeded, watered, plowed, and prayed.

In turn, you should know that your labor of love has not gone unnoticed. You are deeply loved and appreciated – not only by hearts you have tended and cared for, but by the God who made you the mother (and expert gardener) you are.

God bless you, Mom.

There never was a woman like her. She was gentle as a dove and brave as a lioness . . . The memory of my mother and her teachings were, after all, the only capital I had to start life with, and on that capital I have made my way.

—Andrew Jackson

I wanted something more substantial to cut. All of the trees on our place were far too large for me to tackle with my hatchet – all except one.

mother's
cherry tree

My mother loved all growing things. We had apple trees, pear trees, a grape arbor, a rose arbor, tulips, lilacs, irises, and an annual garden. The Merdocks, who lived directly west of us, had a large cherry orchard. Although they gave us all the cherries we wanted, my mother was determined to have her own cherry tree. Accordingly, one fall we planted (I say "we" because I dug the hole) a three-foot sapling. Mother fertilized, watered, watched over, pampered, and stroked that tree until it was a wonder it didn't die from too much attention. It was amazing how it grew, and in its second spring it actually blossomed and bore cherries – not enough to make a pie – but my mother was so proud of the accomplishment that she nearly burst. She even carried some of those cherries in her purse to show her friends.

We always shopped at the A & P grocery store in Royal Oak. Fortunately for me, just down the street was Frentz & Sons Hardware. While my mother shopped, I wandered up and down the aisles of Frentz & Sons. It was a fascinating place. Great bins of nails, rows of hinges, racks of shovels, balls of twine, smells of feed, seed, and leather goods, and a hundred other items all combined to make it a whole world in itself. Inevitably, I was led to the fishing equipment, then the gun rack, and finally to the knife display case. It was a wooden cabinet with a glass door. I stood for long minutes gazing in wonder that there could be so many fine things to be had.

At the bottom of the knife case there was one item in particular that attracted me. It was a belt hatchet – just the right size for me. It had a leather case that could be strapped right onto your belt for carrying purposes. I began to pester my mother about it. One day she actually went in to look at it, and I knew that my pleading was getting somewhere. It was a long process, but eventually she bought it for me.

I remember going around the yard whacking on things. It was exceedingly sharp. I whacked on old two-by-fours, I whacked on an old crate that had been sitting behind the chicken coop – but it was all very dissatisfying. I wanted something more substantial to cut. All of the trees on our place were far too large for me to tackle with my hatchet – all except one – the cherry tree. As preposterous as this seems, the idea was probably enhanced by my school teacher telling us about George Washington cutting down the cherry tree. Since George was quite a hero, the idea of cutting down our cherry tree was an easy step.

I guess that actually walking up and cutting it down all at once was a little too much for me, so I decided to trim it a little first. The result was that I left not a single limb intact. Our cherry tree was reduced to a forlorn looking, tapering rod protruding from the ground. Around its base lay a pile of limbs with the leaves looking limp and sickly.

nurturing hearts

When I stepped back to survey my work, my conscience began speaking to me. You know, consciences are often the most useless things. When I needed it was before I started, but it was completely silent – didn't help me a lick. It never said, "John, you'd best think about this," or "Are you sure this is what you want to do?" *Now,* when it was too late to be of any use whatsoever, here it came – full blast. "Now look what you've done," it cried. Pictures of my mother fertilizing and watering, her proud tones as she displayed those first cherries to all of her friends – all flooded my memory and made me feel terrible.

But what good did it do to feel terrible
after the fact?

I put my hatchet in its case and wandered slowly into the kitchen. I had studied some on how best to approach this situation and had decided that it would be to my best advantage to open the subject before it was discovered.

"I know a little boy who cut down a cherry tree," I piped in my most cheerful, winning voice.

mother's cherry tree

My mother, busily occupied, replied, "Oh, I bet I know who it was. It was George Washington." She said it so nice and sweet that I was reassured and plunged ahead.

"No, it wasn't. It was John Smith."

Right off, there was a noticeable change in both the temperature and the atmospheric pressure in the kitchen. My mother turned on me quickly, and her voice didn't have any sweetness in it – or light either, for that matter.

"Did you cut down my cherry tree?" She grabbed me by my left ear (she was right handed so her grip was better on that side), and we marched out to the scene of the crime – with her nearly lifting me off the ground, using my left ear for leverage.

I would have gone anyway.

When she saw the tree, she started to cry; and since she needed both hands to dry her eyes, she turned loose of my ear – which was a great relief. It was a sad-looking sight – standing there like a little flagpole –

nurturing hearts

but I thought things might go a little easier for me since she was so sad and all. They didn't. She whipped me with every last limb I had chopped off that tree – whipped me till the limb was just shreds of bark left in her hand. I was afraid she was going to start on the pear tree limbs, but she finally gave out. You know, a person is mortally strong when they're aroused like that, and they also have an amazing endurance. It cheered me some to think that she was using the limbs on me instead of the hatchet.

You know, my mother went right back to work on that cherry tree. She kept right on watering and fertilizing and caring for it. Anyone else would have given up. She willed that tree to live, and it did. It grew and became a fine tree with only a few scars on its trunk – to remind me of my folly.

Isn't it amazing how things will grow if they get the right kind of attention? I strongly suspect that there's a lot of folks around right now who were at one time near to death – like mother's cherry tree – because some thoughtless rascal started cutting on them, but now they're healthy and growing because somebody kept watering and fertilizing and loving them – and they lived.

In fact, I strongly suspect that's what happened to me. Today, I am healthy and strong, with only a few scars to remind me of my folly and some folks' attempts to trim me. And I stand here knowing Christ, because both he and my mother wouldn't quit on me.

She willed me to live.
And I live
as a result of her love and determination.

reflections . . .

Today we are all healthy, happy,
moms, wives, sisters, + daughters
because of how you raised us ...

two

shaping
minds

Your teachings have great importance! What you teach guides your children when they walk and watches over them while they sleep. Your instructions are lights for their lives and speak to them even when you aren't there.

Love,
Your God of Wisdom

Proverbs 6:20–23

You may not have a profes-
sional degree, but you are a world-class teacher all
the same. And you practice your profession on a
daily basis – not on a college campus or behind a
podium in a marble-floored classroom – but right
there in the warmth of your carefully kept home.

While you've gone about the rigorous routines
of motherhood, little eyes have watched and little
minds and hearts have been shaped for eternity.
Your young pupils have learned of sacrificial
love as they've seen you take the last and least
so others can have more. They've learned to
distinguish right from wrong as they've
observed your life of honesty and integri-
ty. They've learned about faith as
they've heard you pray to an unseen
God – sometimes in tears, some-

times with thanksgiving, always with a firm
belief that God is real, that he hears your prayers,
and that he responds faithfully. They've learned that
failure is not final as they've seen you confess your
own faults and offer generous forgiveness to others.
Above all, they've learned what real love means – it
means sharing hurts, hopes, joys, and homecomings;
it means staying when it would be easier to leave,
defending when others accuse, holding on when
you're tempted to let go, and letting go when you
desperately want to hold on.

The same lips that have countless times
formed the word "Mom," will say, "Thanks,
Mom, for your precious teachings.
You're the best."

My mother was the most beautiful woman I ever saw. All I am I owe to my mother. I attribute all my success in life to the moral, intellectual and physical education I received from her.

—George Washington

The more I learned, the
more fascinated I became
with my mother's voice
and her moving finger.

learning
to read

My mother taught me to read. She didn't mean to – I mean she wasn't trying to – but she did. I do not know when she began the practice, but I do know that, from my earliest remembrances, she read to me every day before my nap – except Saturday and Sunday. On weekdays, my father was at work and my sister at school, so we would crawl into my parents' bed and prop the pillows up against the iron posts of the bedstead – after fluffing them of course. What a shame that modern children don't even know the word *fluffing*. They don't know it because they don't fluff – you can't fluff polyester and foam rubber. We've added *microchip* to our vocabulary and deleted *fluffing*. It was a sorry exchange, and our language is the more barren for it. Anyway, we would fluff the pillows, nestle back into them, huddle very close to each other, and she would read.

What did she read? The Bible of course – what else? It was the only book in our house. She read stories from the Bible.

She was a finger reader.

When I first read at school, I read the same way; but my teacher, Miss Smoky, absolutely forbade it. I told her my mother read that way, and she said it was okay for my mother but not for me. Miss Smoky was very nice – and she meant well – but I'm really glad that my mother's teacher didn't forbid her to read with her finger because if she had, you see, I wouldn't have learned nearly so soon or so well, and I might not have loved it so.

Oh, you may not know what finger reading is. It's like fluffing, I guess. Finger reading is following the words with your finger so you won't lose your place or jump to the wrong line. It makes perfectly good sense if you think about it. In schools, nowadays, we're very concerned with how fast people read. If you can read a thousand words a minute that is absolutely fantastic –

and it really doesn't matter if you understand the words or enjoy them or take the time to think about them. You must learn to read them very quickly – because there are so many of them – and if you don't read them quickly – my goodness – you may never read all of them. And reading all of them is terribly important, even though most of them aren't worth much.

My mother was a finger reader. Every day as she read, I would hear her voice and watch her finger as it went back and forth across the page. Of course it happened very slowly – and I didn't *know* I was learning to read. I honestly didn't even mean to learn – it was quite an *accident*. I began to associate what my mother was saying with the word above her finger. There were lots of *and*s, *that*s, and *but*s, and I guess I learned those first. It was easy for an uncluttered mind to grasp that it took a long time to say *Belshazzar* and that it also took a lot of letters. The more I learned, the more fascinated I became with my mother's voice and her moving finger.

shaping minds

One day I corrected her. She either mispronounced or skipped a word – I don't remember which – and I corrected her. She was incredulous. "How did you know that?" she asked. I didn't know how I knew. I just knew that the word she said wasn't the word that was above her finger. I did not know the alphabet – that would come much later in school. I didn't know phonics – I still don't – but I could tell a telephone pole from a fire hydrant, and I could tell the difference between Jehu and Jerusalem. My mother asked me to read, and I did it gladly – slowly, haltingly – finger under the words. With her coaching, I read. Then I read with no coaching, and we took turns. Mom read one day – I read the next.

When I went to school a couple of years later, Miss Smokey tried to teach me to read. I told her I could already read. I could tell it hurt her feelings, so I said I was sorry – but reading was a piece of cake. They were reading Dick and Jane, and I knew Nebuchadnezzar, Jebusite, Perizzite, Shamgar, and Rehoboam. I told her she could teach me math –

I was real dumb in that.

learning to read

But I want you to see – that if my mother was teaching me to read – without meaning to – she was also teaching me about God, about right and wrong, about good and evil. Yes, those ideas were forming in my mind – waiting for the moment when I would need them to help me understand my growing, changing world.

She didn't mean to – any more than she meant to teach me to read. She read the Bible because she loved to read the Bible – because it had great meaning to her. If I hadn't been around, she would have read it anyway; and after I went to school and didn't take naps anymore, she continued to read. She only knew that it entertained me and that it was good for me in some general way.

Again, my specific point is that both teaching me to read and teaching me about God – about good and evil and standing for the right – did not come to me through lectures and sermons – although I heard plenty of them at church – they came to me through my mother's attempt to establish and strengthen her own relationship with God.

shaping minds

Her daily awareness of his providence,
her constant devotion to his will,
her love for his word –
passed to me – *naturally.*

reflections . . .

You have taught us all so many things - as children, teenagers, and adults ... thank you!

three

imparting faith

*F*an the flame of my gift in your children. Sincere faith can be passed on to your children and to their children from generation to generation. Keep passing on a heritage of faith. Don't let my flame go out!

Love,

Your 100% Faithful God

2 Timothy 1:5

When it comes to matters of eternity, moms have a special sense. Somehow moms can see beyond disheveled hair, freshly torn jeans, and smudged faces. Moms can look into the tearful eyes of an unhappy two-year-old or the questioning eyes of a moody teenager and see not only what is – but what can be.

As you interact with your children in your daily routines – routines that may seem mundane and far removed from eternity – remember that you are imparting a sense of something much bigger than the here and now. You are imparting seeds of faith. As your children watch you react to sadness, joy, tragedy, success, and failure, they begin to learn what it means to have faith in something beyond themselves.

Your gentle reassurance when things go wrong, your unfailing confidence in the face of apparent failure, your ability to trust God when life seems to be falling apart – these responses give faith structure and meaning. You are the "embodiment" of faith – faith "with skin on."

Every new day presents opportunities to pass on little bits of your faith – little bits of eternity. Enjoy a beautiful sunset together and remind your children of the God who made it. Use the death of a loved one to talk about heaven. When hearts get broken or dreams fall apart, remind them that God holds the key to real happiness and that he is the rebuilder of hopes and dreams. When uncertainty clouds their vision, lead them to their knees in prayer – pray with them often and about everything. When Satan wins a battle, wrap your arms around them, gently embrace confidence back into them, and tell them of God's unconditional love – a love that will love them no matter what.

When it comes to matters of eternity . . . moms have a special sense.

I believe the most
valuable contribution
a parent can make to
his child is to instill
in him a genuine
faith in God.

—Dr. James Dobson

Sometimes – on Mother's Day, especially – I miss her till I ache. I miss her steadfast faith in a loving God, and I wish I could lay my head in her lap and she would stroke my hair and soothe my fears.

mother's day

mother's day

In 1944 our country was engaged in world war. I was seven. A member of our family had been killed at Pearl Harbor, so the war was very real to us. My mother read daily newspaper accounts of death tolls and of battles won and lost. It was a frightening time.

My father worked long hours at a converted Chrysler automobile factory – now simply called *The Tank Arsenal.* He did not get home till very late at night. Because we lived in a rural setting, my mother was often apprehensive during his absence and refused to go to bed until he got home – and so we passed the time by singing. My mother would play the piano, and she and my sister and I would sing. We sang "Red River Valley," "You Are My Sunshine," and "I've Been Working on the Railroad." We sang church songs too – "Sweet Hour of

imparting faith

Prayer" and "When We All Get to Heaven." My father was from Arkansas, and he had taught us some deep south songs, like "Old Kentucky Home," "The Camptown Races," and "Old Black Joe."

One night, after singing long, I went to bed before my father came home. The song "Old Black Joe" remained on my mind.

> Gone are the days
> When my heart was young and gay.
> Gone are my friends
> From the cotton field away.
> Gone from the earth
> To a better land I know.
> I hear their gentle voices calling,
> "Old Black Joe."
> "I'm commin', I'm commin',
> For my head is bending low,"
> I hear their gentle voices calling,
> "Old Black Joe."

I don't know why that song made such a profound impression on me – maybe it was the war and thoughts of death – or maybe it was the uncertainty we all felt – but my child's heart was moved. I felt so sad for Old Black Joe that I began to cry, and the more I cried, the harder I cried. My mother heard me and came to my room. She sat on the bed in the dark and stroked my head and held me. She asked me what was wrong, and I told her I didn't like that song about Old Black Joe because it made me think about dead people and sad things, and I thought he must have been terribly mis-treated to be so sad.

She told me that there was much grief in the world and much injustice. She said that dying wasn't always such a bad thing – that sometimes it was better than liv-ing. She said that Old Black Joe wanted to be with his friends and that now he was – that heaven was a nice place and that God had a very special place for Old Black Joe and his friends and that they were hav-ing a good time together.

I went to sleep so happy for Old Black Joe and loving God, who was so nice to him. I was glad that Old Black Joe was

imparting faith

having a good life there, because he had such a bad one here. I really believed what my mother told me. I trusted her completely. It was the foundation of my faith, and I still believe it

to this very day.

Sometimes – on Mother's Day, especially – I miss her till I ache. I miss her steadfast faith in a loving God, and I wish I could lay my head in her lap and she would stroke my hair and soothe my fears. I believe that God has a special place for her and that she and her friends are happy and singing with Old Black Joe and his friends.

For I am mindful of the sincere faith within you,
which first dwelt in your grandmother, Lois,
and in your mother, Eunice,
and I am sure
that it is in you as well.
—2 Timothy 1:5

reflections . . .

Because of the loss of your own Mom + Dad you've taught us to appreciate each day + enjoy what we have. You're such a great Grandma to the kids – how lucky we all are . . .

four

giving
encouragement

*E*ncourage and build up your family daily. Help them identify and get rid of everything that hinders them and the sin that so easily entangles them. Challenge them to run with endurance the race of life I've already marked out for them. Give them courage!

Love,

Your God Who Gives You
Endurance and Encouragement

1 Thessalonians 5:11
Hebrews 3:13; 12:1
Romans 15:5

A word of encouragement from Mom takes the *im* out of *impossible,* the *'t* out of *can't,* and the *un* out of *unable.* A cheerful word from Mom can turn impending failure into success and can spur a child on to finish a seemingly impossible task.

This world can be a frightening place – classroom assignments, playground bullies, music recitals, term papers, competitive sports – such challenges often require the courage of David facing Goliath. And sometimes the weight of it all feels like heavy weights around the ankles.

At times like these, children – both young and old – need the gift of courage. And that's what *encouragers* do – they impart *courage* –

and moms are some of the best encouragers
in the world. Just a few simple words from you
give your children courage to meet the challenges at
hand: "I believe in you." "You can do it." "You are so
special." "I am so proud of you." "Keep going . . .
keep fighting . . . keep believing."

This world is full of people and events that drain
faith and spirit from your family, but God has given
you the ability to fight off these enemies with loving
words of encouragement. Never underestimate
their power.

Watch your children's backs straighten,
their eyes brighten, their work improve, their
lives change, and their love deepen – all
because you have imparted courage
to them by your words.

*E*very time we
encourage someone,
we give them a
transfusion of
courage.

—Charles Swindoll

There were hundreds of people crowding in, shouting and screaming, but this mother was determined to be heard. "Run, Tami, run – Run, Tami, run," she pleaded.

run, tami, run

I have a dear friend who lives in Dallas, and he has a daughter who is a very talented runner. The regional cross-country championships were held in my town, and he called to ask if I could pick up his wife from the airport and give her a place to stay while she was there to watch their daughter run. I was delighted to do it and so I found myself on Saturday morning witnessing the Texas Regional Cross-Country Races at Mae Simmons Park. I witnessed something there – a wonderful, moving thing – a thing of beauty worth telling and retelling.

It was a marvelously bright, clear, cool morning, and hundreds of spectators had gathered on the hillsides to watch. They were mostly family members who had traveled many miles – in some cases, hundreds of miles – to watch just one race. I had no child running, and so I found myself watching those who did. Their faces were intent, their eyes always picking out the only runner they were interested in; and often, when the runners were far away and could not hear their shouts of encouragement, still their lips would move, mouthing the precious, familiar names – and *one other word.* Sometimes they said the names audibly, but softly, as if for no ears but their own, and yet it seemed that they hoped to be heard.

"*Run,* Jimmy," they whispered urgently.
"*Run,* Tracy."
"*Run.*"

The cross-country race is two miles for girls, three for boys. It is a grueling run – physically and mentally exhausting – over hills and rough terrain. There were ten races that morning, beginning with class 1A boys and girls and ending with class 5A boys and girls. Each race had from eighty to one hundred twenty competitors. The course ended where it began, but at times the runners were nearly a half-mile away.

As the class 5A girl's race came to a close, I watched a forty-plus-year-old mother – who was wearing patent leather shoes and a skirt and carrying a purse – run the last hundred yards beside her daughter. She saw no other runners. As she ran awkwardly – her long dark hair coming undone and streaming out behind her, giving no thought to the spectacle she made – she cried, *"Run,* Tami, *run! – Run,* Tami, *run!"* There were hundreds of people crowding in, shouting and screaming, but this mother was determined to be heard. *"Run,* Tami, *run – Run,* Tami, *run,"* she pleaded. The girl had no chance to win, and the voice of her mother, whose heart was bursting with exertion and emotion, was not urging her to win.

She was urging her to finish.

The girl was in trouble. Her muscles were cramping; her breath came in ragged gasps; her stride was broken, faltering; she was in the last stages of weariness – just before collapse. But when she heard her mother's voice, a marvelous transformation took place. She straightened, she found her balance, her bearing, her rhythm; and she finished. She crossed the finish line, turned, and collapsed into the arms of her mother.

They fell down together on the grass and they cried, and then they laughed. They were having the best time together, like there was no one else in the world but them. "God," I thought, "that is so beautiful. Thank you for letting me see that."

As I drove away from Mae Simmons Park, I couldn't get it off my mind. A whole morning of outstanding performances had merged into a single happening. I thought of my own children and of a race they are running – a different and far more important race. A race that requires even greater stamina, courage, and character. I am a spectator in that race also. I have helped them to train, I have pleaded – instructed – threatened – punished – prayed – praised – laughed – and cried. I have even tried to familiarize them with the course. But now the gun is up, and their race has begun, and I am a spectator. My heart is bursting –

I see no other runners.

run, tami, run

Sometimes their course takes them far from me, and yet I whisper, *"Run,* children, *run."* They do not hear, but there is One who does. Occasionally, they grow weary, because the race is long and demands such sacrifice. They witness hypocrisy, and there are many voices that call to them to quit this foolish race, telling them they cannot possibly win. They lose sight of their goal and they falter, stumble – and I cry,

"Run, children, *run* – Oh God – please *run."*

And then they come to the last hundred yards – how I long to be there, to run beside them. *"Run,* Lincoln; *run,* Debbie; *run,* Brendan; *run,* Kristen. What if I am gone, and there is no one to whisper, to shout *"Run"* in their ears? What if Satan convinces them that they are not going to win? What if his great lie – that you must beat the others – causes them to allow defeat to settle over them? What if they lose sight of the great truth – that in this race, it is *finishing* that is the victory. That is why our Lord Jesus said at the last,

"It is finished."

giving encouragement

And that is why the great apostle Paul said,

"I have finished my course."

Dear Lord Jesus,
As you have run beside me,
Please run beside them.
Strengthen their knees
That they might finish.

And dear Father,
When they cross that eternal finish line –
May I be there to
welcome them home.
May we laugh and cry
through eternity –
Praising the grace that
gave us this victory.

Run, Tami – *Run.*

reflections . . .

In your own gentle way - you
always encouraged us ... with me it
was in school + in basketball ...
never pushing but always a source
of courage, love, + accomplishment -
you helped me realize I could
do it!

sharing laughter

*L*ighten up! Laughter is good medicine—it's a great "shock absorber" for life's bumps. Don't miss out on the continual feast of a cheerful heart. A happy heart makes your face cheerful.

Love,

Your God of Joy

Proverbs 17:22; 15:13–15

You know the scenario – and it's not a pretty sight. The day begins badly. Tension fills the house. The family is at each other's throats. Even the family pet seems to have an attitude. An argument starts. Tempers flare. Accusations fly. Violence erupts as a deadly pillow is thrown across the room.

Who can remedy this deplorable situation? Who can rescue the day? Who can restore peace, order, and the American way? Who, who, who? Only one person can bring this chaos under control – you – Super Mom.

And what weaponry will you use to stop this rushing wall of tension that threatens all of mankind? Laughter. You find the humor in the moment, and you laugh. When Mom laughs, everyone laughs.

If joy is good medicine, then the laughter of a mom is a miracle cure. It short-circuits the temper, drowns the fires of tension, and calms the tempest.

A heavy air of tension covers our society. It can seep into the home and poison the air before you know what's happening. But it cannot infiltrate a home filled with laughter. So laugh a lot. Look for the lighter side. Your laughter is infectious – it heals and refreshes. It reminds the family that things are never as bad as they may seem.

Where there is laughter, hope can grow. Where there is hope, faith thrives. Where there is faith, the Savior reigns. Where the Savior rules the heart, joy is made complete. Let his love live in you richly, and laughter will come easily.

No. You will not be able to leap tall buildings in a single bound, but you will be able to lift your family above the daily struggles of life.

Say, do you always wear that cape around the house?

*I*f you can't make
it better, you can
laugh at it.

—Erma Bombeck

I should have known better. There was something in his voice that said, "Don't ask Mom," but my frustration overcame my better judgement.

saturday morning

I still can't believe it really happened. I was steamed about it for weeks after. I – well – let me start from the beginning.

Saturday mornings are special. They're meant for late, great breakfasts, for walking around the neighborhood, for getting and contributing to the local gossip, for running unimportant errands, and for just being lazy in general. They seldom work out that way – but that's what they're for.

I had my schedule all worked out. I would leave at 7:40, get to the post office when it opened at 8:00, mail my packages, leave at 8:15, arrive at the appliance dealer at 8:30, get the part I needed for the washing machine, and be home by 9:00. I should finish the repair job by 9:30 and have the rest of my Saturday to while away in the appropriate fashion that I described above.

It all started wonderfully. I got up – and I *almost* left on time; however, as I bounced energetically up the post office steps whistling "Yankee Doodle," I came face-to-face with a sign that read, "Closed on Saturdays." My shock and chagrin were indescribable. The good old, ever-lovin', dependable – rain, shine, sleet, and snow – post office was not open!

I was frosted.

Just shows what shape this country's in. Man, back in '47, when *I* worked for the post office, back in *the good old days* when men were men and women were . . . sweet potatoes – well, something different than what they are now – anyway, back then, the post office opened at 8:00 A.M. sharp, *every day* – except of course – Sundays; and we knew that nothing ought to be open on Sundays – except of course – churches and Big Daddy's Delightful Diner.

I shuffled back to the car, muttering under my breath – words too wonderful for language – my schedule shot, my whole morning thrown out of rhythm. I bought a copy of the local paper – to pass some time before the appliance store opened.

Finally, the appliance store opened. I ran in and got my part and drove home. By the time I arrived, I was in no mood to be trifled with. I was looking for some new family atrocity as an excuse to vent my anger. As I walked in the house, my son asked me if I had gotten a new window pane for his bedroom. Of course I hadn't – I didn't even know it was broken. Here was the opportunity I was looking for.

"I don't know how you managed to do something so stupid, but you are going to pay for it, young man." I said in an angry, threatening tone –

I was feeling better already.

"I didn't break it, honest, Dad," he replied hurriedly.

"Where is your brother hiding?"

"He didn't do it either."

"Then who did?" My exasperation was rising to a dangerous level.

sharing laughter

"Ask Mom."

I should have known better. There was something in his voice that said, *"Don't ask Mom,"* but my frustration overcame my better judgement.

"Judi!!!" I yelled, "Where are you?"

She said, "Don't yell; I'm right here. What do you want?"

"I want to know – and I want to know *right now* – who broke this window?"

I spoke in my most intimidating tone – a tone that is calculated to cause the children to run to their rooms and cower in mortal terror under their beds – a tone that is calculated to make their mother cringe and grovel in submission and to speak with the utmost deference for my authority.

"I did," she said. She not only didn't grovel, but there was a definite lack of humility, or even apology, in her tone. In fact, what she said was, "Do you want to make an issue out of this, Buster? Because if you do, I am ready to take some of that *'Blessed Assurance'* out of you."

saturday morning

Still angry, but with some restraint, I asked, "How did you do that?"

"*If* it's any of your business," she began in a very defensive tone that said that it most certainly was *not* any of my business, "it was one of those perfectly normal things that could have happened to anybody –

I was killing a fly."

She stopped there as though that was a perfectly sensible, adequate, and complete explanation. I knew I was treading on dangerous soil, but I plunged ahead. "I don't completely understand exactly how those two things go together," I said timidly.

"Well," she said, with disgust dripping from her voice, "I should have known that it was useless for a *woman* to try to explain anything to a *man*. I suppose I'll have to tell you the whole story."

Very meekly, I apologized for my stupidity and begged her to indulge me.

"Well, after you left, I decided to make a pumpkin pie. I had just taken it out of the oven and placed it on the counter to cool. When I went back to check on it, there was a fly walking around on it. That made my blood boil. I tried to shoo it away, but it wouldn't move, so I rolled up a newspaper and hit it. I missed the fly, but I splattered pumpkin pie all over the kitchen. That *really* made me mad. I chased the fly into Lincoln's bedroom, and it landed on the window. I couldn't hit it with the newspaper because it had pumpkin pie on it and I didn't want to mess up the window, so I took off my shoe and bashed his stupid, miserable brains out with the heel, which broke the stupid, miserable window. Now doesn't that make perfectly good sense?"

As I stood there looking at the broken window, I began to get tickled. The more I thought about my wife, seething with rage, bent upon destruction, hounding her quarry unmercifully – until in desperation, the helpless creature, gasping for breath, abandoned any hope of escape and landed on a window, only to be smashed by a shoe – the funnier it all seemed; and right then I needed a laugh.

saturday morning

I assured my wife that it made perfectly good sense. I applauded her determination and judgement and went to the hardware store to buy a new window.

I laughed for a week.

The moral of this story depends on who you are. If you're a fly, the moral is don't land on pumpkin pies or window panes. If you're a man, the moral is that women are fearsome things and neither their pies nor their logic are to be trifled with. If you're a woman, the moral is that men's egos are very fragile and their bark is worse than their bite, so at least *act* a little submissive now and then. I think that the overall moral is that first – Saturday mornings were meant for special things and anybody who messes with the divine plan is placing his life, health, and eternal happiness in great danger; second – it's good to laugh – laughter will lengthen your life span, improve your marriage, increase your humility and your appreciation, and make your testimony for Jesus more believable.

reflections . . .

I love what is says on page 79. You always knew how to make days special & I do remember laughing a lot!

valuing
motherhood

You are worth far more than rubies! You lack nothing of value. You bring good to every day. You work vigorously, and your life is profitable. You are clothed with strength and dignity! You can laugh at life. You speak with wisdom and faithful instruction; you juggle numerous roles and use your time wisely. Your children arise and call you blessed and your husband also praises you! Many women do noble things, but you surpass them all! Others also see what you do and admire your work as a Mom.

Love,
Your God Who Praises You
for Fearing Me

Proverbs 31:10–30

I have an important message for you. It may come as a surprise, because this message is not repeated nearly often enough. Are you ready?

You are greatly admired. It's worth repeating. You are *greatly* admired.

And not just by your family – by others, too. Some of your admirers are close acquaintances, others are strangers; but they all hold you in high regard. Why? Because you are a mother through and through, in and out, and all about.

Because you are totally in love with your family and are thoroughly prepared to show your love by giving all, asking little, and accepting less. Because you can find joy in a Saturday morning filled with scampering feet, raucous laughter, and a house straightened just yesterday and strewn with toys today. Because you have become an expert at being in three places at one time, because you are a tender nurse beside the bed of a sick child, because you are a diplomatic disciplinarian, because you are a mighty warrior against the forces of evil that threaten your home. Because you see the amazing potential in the hearts and minds of awkward, and sometimes annoying, boys and girls.

Please disregard any previous message you may have received that gave the impression that you were not highly valued and greatly respected. You are a rich and treasured gift from God. You may do many other things in your life on earth that will be productive and meaningful, but none will be as admired as being the beautiful mother you are.

Who ran to help me when I fell

And would some pretty story tell,

Or kiss the place to make it well?

My mother.

—Ann Taylor

It was an important
moment – a critical
moment – and more was
riding on it than anybody
who was watching could
possibly have known.

the redhead and the brunette

They sat right in front of me on a Southwest flight. Those of you who have flown on Southwest know how close that is – I could smell their perfume. I think they were about the same age and the same build –

but all similarity vanished at that point.

The brunette arrived first. She was beautifully, stylishly, immaculately dressed. Everything matched. Her hair was radiant, there were subtle changes of color when she moved her head, and the light shone from any angle with vibrant intensity. Every strand was in place. Her nails were long and manicured, her lipstick and makeup were flawless, and she was breathtakingly beautiful. She carried a very smart-looking, soft-leather briefcase, which must have cost a small fortune, and inside it, she had a powerbook. She was also carrying an exclusive looking shopping bag that had "Macy's" written in large letters on one side.

She had a beautiful smile – a radiant smile that lit up her whole face. She parted her lips slowly, invitingly, and revealed perfect, white, even teeth. It was a deliberate smile – one that she had practiced before the mirror a thousand times. She wore three rings. They weren't the large, gaudy kind, they were the stylish, expensive-looking kind. Two of the rings were on her right hand, and one was on her left. There was no ring on her "ring finger." She placed the shopping bag in an overhead compartment, and sat down in the window seat with her briefcase.

The redhead was carrying a huge diaper bag, a fold-up stroller, and a baby. Her hair was all over her head, not unkempt, but frazzled. Her clothes were modest, they fit loosely on her spare frame, and they had "K-Mart" written all over them. She wore no makeup, and she carried no shopping bag. Her nails were so short that they couldn't be manicured, and she only wore one ring. It was on her "ring finger" – and it wasn't expensive. She smiled at the brunette and asked if she could sit next to her. She had a great smile. It was one of those smiles that just explodes – nobody could ever hope to practice a smile like that. It happened so quickly that you couldn't tell where it started, but before it was over, it had gotten into her eyes, magnified the dimples in her cheeks, wrinkled her nose, lifted her eyebrows, raised her ears, showed the fillings in her teeth – and whether you wanted to or not, you found yourself smiling back.

At first, you could tell that the brunette didn't want to be bothered, but the smile did it. She couldn't possibly resist that smile. She smiled back, a little stiffly, and said she would be glad for her to sit next to her. And she said it with so much friendly enthusiasm

that I think she surprised herself.

We hadn't seen the baby yet, but as soon as the mother sat down, the baby stuck her head out from under the blanket. She was (I say "she" because she "looked" like a she) about nine months to a year old, I think, and she was the absolute image of her mother – I mean there was no doubt whose baby this was – she even had the same explosive smile.

The redhead was bubbly and excited. I picked up enough of the conversation to know that she had been to see her mother, who had never seen the baby, and she had had a great visit, but she was anxious to get home and see her husband. The brunette was all business. She wasn't unfriendly exactly, but she spoke in clipped, precise tones. She stated her name, her company, her position, the colleges she had attended – told the redhead that her baby was cute – opened her briefcase, took out her powerbook, turned it on, and began scanning some documents in a way that was calculated to let the redhead know that the conversation was over.

But the redhead didn't take the cue.

The redhead was cute, really cute, and she possessed an innate type of enthusiasm and innocence that unsettled the brunette. She chatted easily and naturally about her husband, her house, and her neighbors, and she told the brunette all the plans she had for the baby's room. She was breast-feeding the baby, and it came time to eat. The brunette watched in absolute amazement as the redhead very easily and modestly made arrangements for feeding the baby. While the baby was eating, the mother needed something and asked the brunette if she would mind getting it for her out of the diaper bag. The brunette closed the powerbook, placed it in the leather briefcase, zipped it up, and reached for the diaper bag.

Ten minutes later, the baby was through eating and was ready to play. The mother placed the baby over her shoulder and patted her on the back until she burped. The brunette watched. After the burp, the baby sat on the redhead's lap and cooed, gurgled, grabbed everything in sight, and tried to stuff whatever she grabbed into her mouth. The brunette never took her eyes off of the redhead and the baby.

The baby, smiling at the brunette, was captivated by her dangling, colorful earring and reached for it. The mother grabbed the hand just in time and said, "No! No!"

valuing motherhood

The brunette assured her it was all right, took the earring off, and handed it to the baby – who immediately put it in her mouth. The mother rescued the earring, gently mentioned that it wasn't good to give the baby articles that could be swallowed, and handed the earring back.

"Would you mind if I held her?" I couldn't believe my ears. It was the brunette. ("This ought to be good," I said to myself.)

"My goodness, no. I don't mind at all, but are you sure you want to? She squirms a lot, and she will wrinkle your clothes – and," she added, with a touch of admiration in her voice, "your clothes are so beautiful."

The brunette tentatively held out her hands toward the baby, absolutely convinced, I'm sure, that the baby would reject her. I thought she would too. It was an important moment, a critical moment, and more was riding on it than anybody who was watching could possibly be aware of. The baby looked hesitantly at the extended hands, then looked tentatively at the mother, who smiled reassuringly, then that smile exploded all over the baby's face, and she reached out both of her hands toward the brunette. It was great.

The brunette placed the baby's face right next to hers and held her so tight I thought the baby would cry. She was a little stiff at first, but it didn't take her long to get the hang of it; and before long, she was doing it like an old pro. I couldn't see the brunette's face, but I knew the look of peace and joy that was on it. For the next twenty minutes, this perfectly dressed woman cooed, baby talked, patted, played "patty cake," bounced, and entertained the baby.

After about ten minutes, the baby threw up – I think "spit up" is more accurate. The redhead was horrified and tried to clean it up with a diaper. She apologized all over herself and reached to take the baby back. The brunette – to her credit – was gracious and assured her that she didn't care, and she insisted on keeping the baby.

When the captain announced that we were on our final approach, the redhead took the baby back, and the brunette

valuing motherhood

got out her makeup kit and spent the rest of the time restoring her businesslike, pristine appearance. When we got off the plane, the brunette offered to carry the baby to the baggage claim area, and the redhead said she would be grateful. The redhead put the Macy's shopping bag, the diaper bag, and the leather briefcase in the fold-up stroller, and they chatted on the most intimate terms all the way to baggage claim. I followed closely, determined to see how this was going to play out.

The redhead's husband was waiting for her at baggage claim, and after they had kissed and hugged each other for an inordinately long time, she introduced the brunette, who reluctantly handed the baby to the father. As they waited for their luggage to come, the redhead and her husband stood close together, with their arms around each other – the father holding the baby. Once, the baby reached for the brunette. She started to reach back, but checked herself, and with some effort, deliberately placed her hands at her sides.

The redhead's luggage came first. The husband picked up the bags, and the redhead turned to say goodbye. The brunette and the redhead hugged each other in a genuine, spontaneous display of emotion. Then the brunette picked up the Macy's bag and handed it to the redhead, pleading with her to take it. I couldn't hear all of the conversation, but it was obvious that they were both embarrassed. The brunette won, and the Macy's bag was added to the other luggage. Then the brunette reached out, placed her fingers softly on the cheek of the baby, and whispered some parting affection to her.

Just before they disappeared, she waved goodbye to the baby, whose face was toward her, and the baby made a gesture that might have been interpreted as a farewell wave. When the brunette turned back toward the luggage carousel, there were tears and makeup smudges on both cheeks. She made no attempt to wipe them away. Her luggage came. She got a cart and placed her luggage on it.

She stood a long moment, wiped the tears and smudges with her fingers – making them worse, of course – gathered herself,

valuing motherhood

grabbed the cart handles, and walked determinedly toward the exit.

The redhead, I imagine, went back to her home and the brunette back to her office – both, I feel quite sure – feeling more keenly

the value of mothering.

reflections . . .

Mom - motherhood - no one can prepare
you for the challenges, ups, downs,
heartaches, + awesome pride you feel
(all in the matter of minutes) But
you did teach us to be good moms
through example... what a lesson,
what sacrifices you made...

seven

building memories

*P*ass on "roots" to your children. Remember the days of old; consider the generations long past. Meditate on all my works, and consider what I have done for you.

Love,

Your Lord of Your Heritage

Deuteronomy 32:7
Psalm 143:5

You have a special ability

that you may not even be aware of. In fact, you may have even exercised that ability today. You have the ability to *make memories.* Some memories leave deep, lasting impressions that impact crucial decisions and attitudes. Others produce only a small ripple – a ripple that moves gently through the heart, almost undetected – yet the future often notes its significance.

It's true that some memories "just happen" – like the humorous memory of the recipe you thought would be soooo good that actually turned out to be a disaster, or the horrific memory of Mom running over the family cat, or the sweet, enduring memory of your special perfume.

But I'm talking about *purposeful* memories – traditions that instill a sense of family and an assurance of love: holiday singing (it doesn't matter whether you can carry a tune), family vacations, talent nights, bedtime prayers, special uninterrupted times when the whole family sits down together and talks about what's going on in their lives.

God's Word is filled with "rememberings" – "Remember our covenant, remember your commitment, remember my commands, remember the Christ." And God set up special traditions to cement these memories in the minds of his people. You can do the same thing.

You may hear occasional protests concerning these events. Don't listen. Rest assured that one day you will hear these rewarding words, "Remember when we did that, Mom? That was really a special time, wasn't it?"

You can be a memory-making mom.

I remember, I remember
The house where I was born,
The little window where the sun
Came peeping in at morn.

—Thomas Hood

Sometimes when I came
in to get a drink or some
needed thing or to ask if I
could go farther than normal, she would say, "John,
come here and sing this
with me."

my mother
played the piano

My mother played the piano. She played mostly by ear, I think, but she often looked at the notes too. She played "Red River Valley," "When My Blue Moon Turns to Gold Again," and "Mexicali Rose" – but mostly she played church songs. My dad was a member of a church-song book club, of some sort, and they were always sending us a new songbook. My dad would sit in his chair for hours singing, "do-so-mi-do," as he tried to learn all the songs in the new book.

My mom played them on the piano.

As I remember, she mostly played in the early or mid-afternoon. During those summer months, I would approach our little white house, and through the open

building memories

windows, with the white curtains moving with the breeze, I would hear her playing and singing. It was a very comforting – reassuring – sound. I'm sure it brought much happiness to her.

Sometimes when I came in to get a drink or some needed thing or to ask if I could go farther than normal, she would say, "John, come here and sing this with me." She didn't say it like a command or an order or anything – not like when she said, "Go clean the chicken coop," or "Go hoe the garden." Those were orders. She would just say it like a request or like she would appreciate it as a favor – you know. I usually didn't want to. I was afraid my friends would hear through the open windows – or worse yet they would say, "What took you so long?" And I would sort of cringe and say, "I was singing some church songs with my mother," and they would look at me as though my driveway didn't go all the way to the street.

I made every possible excuse I could. Of course, I didn't just say *no*. You can't do that with requests, you know, and besides, I didn't say that word to my parents.

my mother played the piano

The "N" word was the death word, and if I said it –
even in fun – I would die.

I always knew that.

"Come on John," she would coax, "it will only take
a minute."

"Oh Mom," I would say, "Oh, *Mother*" – the exasperation and disgust would absolutely drip from my
voice, but usually I would go, dragging my reluctant
feet.

She would be so enthusiastic. She would say, "Now,
I want you to sing this alto part for me." And she would
play it and sing it, and then she would play it while I
sang it. Then she would play the soprano part and sing
that – then she would play both of them and sing my
part – and then she would play both parts, and I
would sing alto while she sang soprano. You can't
imagine how excited she would be when we finished. "Isn't that just the prettiest song you ever
heard?" she would exclaim. If I thought it
was something less than that –

I certainly kept it to myself.

building memories

I played my role halfheartedly – at best. I had learned that the quickest way back outside was to learn my part as rapidly as possible, but sometimes I just couldn't get into it and sang so poorly and was so sour-faced and sullen that she would slowly close the book, pat me on the shoulder and say, "You go on back to your friends now. We'll do this some other time."

Although I was a reluctant participant, the memories of playing the piano with my mother are among my sweetest. Sometimes now, when I can find a place where it is still and allow myself to be very quiet, I can see the old white house with the white curtains moving at the open windows; and through those open windows, I hear her voice and see those nimble fingers moving on the keys.

"From this valley they say you are going,
we will miss your bright eyes and sweet smile,
for they say you are taking the sunshine
that has brightened our path for awhile."

"Come on, John," she coaxes,
"it will only take a minute.

my mother played the piano

You sing alto – it goes like this –
and I'll sing soprano –
Isn't that the most beautiful song you ever heard?"

And in my mind I say, "I'm coming, Mom," and I
rush to her with joy, because I know how happy it will
make her.

And it is, you know,
the most beautiful song
I ever heard.

reflections . . .

We made lots of memories . . .

tandem rides, going to Gr.
and Gr. Cable's house, ice skating
on Shinneman Dr., playing "Go to
Jail", haunted houses in the
basement, climbing in bed with
you on stormy nights . . .